PIUTE MIDDLE SCHOOL
Lancaster School District
44711 N. Cedar Ave.
Lancaster, CA 93534

Selman Waksman and the Discovery of Streptomycin

Karen Gordon

Mitchell Lane
PUBLISHERS

PO Box 619 • Bear, Delaware 19701
www.mitchelllane.com

Unlocking the Secrets of Science

Profiling 20th Century Achievers in Science, Medicine, and Technology

Selman Waksman and the Discovery of Streptomycin

Library of Congress Cataloging-in-Publication Data
Gordon, Karen, 1976-
    Selman Waksman and the discovery of streptomycin/Karen Gordon.
       p. cm. (Unlocking the secrets of science)
    Summary: Describes the life and career of Selman Waksman, the microbiologist and chemist who discovered streptomycin and first coined the term "antibiotic."
    Includes bibliographical references and index.
    ISBN 1-58415-138-2
    1. Waksman, Selman A. (Selman Abraham), 1888-1973—Juvenile literature. 2. Microbiologists—Biography—Juvenile literature. 3. Streptomycin—History—Juvenile literature. [1. Waksman, Selman A. (Selman Abraham), 1888-1973. 2. Microbiologists. 3. Scientists. 4. Streptomycin—History. 5. Nobel Prizes—Biography.]
    I. Title. II. Series.
    QR31.W3 G67 2002
    579'.092—dc21
    [B]   2002023652

ABOUT THE AUTHOR: A former associate editor at *Tiger Beat* magazine, Karen Gordon has been writing biographies for young adults for several years. As an editorial assistant and freelance writer, she has written and edited magazine articles. This is her first book for Mitchell Lane.

CHILDREN'S SCIENCE REVIEW EDITOR: Stephanie Kondrchek, B.S. Microbiology, University of Maryland

PHOTO CREDITS: cover: p. 6 Rutgers University; p. 10 (left) Hulton/Archive; (right) Corbis; p. 11 Corbis; p. 12 Rutgers University Archives; p. 18 Corbis; p. 24 Corbis; p. 26 AP; p. 30 Rutgers University Archives; p. 32 Hulton/Archive; p. 34 Rutgers University Archives; p. 37 Corbis; p. 38 Corbis; p. 40 Rutgers University

PUBLISHER'S NOTE: In selecting those persons to be profiled in this series, we first attempted to identify the most notable accomplishments of the 20th century in science, medicine, and technology. When we were done, we noted a serious deficiency in the inclusion of women. For the greater part of the 20th century science, medicine, and technology were male-dominated fields. In many cases, the contributions of women went unrecognized. Women have tried for years to be included in these areas, and in many cases, women worked side by side with men who took credit for their ideas and discoveries. Even as we move forward into the 21st century, we find women still sadly underrepresented. It is not an oversight, therefore, that we profiled mostly male achievers. Information simply does not exist to include a fair selection of women.

Contents

Selman Waksman found the first effective treatment for tuberculosis in a place no one had thought to look—he found it in dirt.

Chapter 1
The White Plague

• •

It has many nicknames. Consumption. The Captain of the Men of Death. The Great White Death. The Great White Plague. The People's Plague. The King's Evil. The World Wide Dread.

It is tuberculosis, which for many centuries killed more human beings than any other disease. More than bubonic plague. More than smallpox. More than cancer.

The unique and terrifying thing about tuberculosis is that it comes in many different forms and can attack the body in various ways. Its most common symptoms are high fever, significant weight loss, and the chronic coughing up of bright red arterial blood. But what makes it so tragic is the very slow pace of its destruction. This is why it was once known as consumption, because the bodies of its victims slowly wasted away. They grew very pale as their decline continued, which was why people also called it the White Plague.

The fear of tuberculosis plagued the minds of the healthy. It was always lurking in the shadows, a constant threat. Those first telltale symptoms—the lingering, harsh cough, the coughing up of bright red blood—inspired terror. Everybody knew somebody who had it. Famous artists, literary and political figures suffered from it. The writers Charlotte and Emily Bronte, Anton Chekhov, D.H. Lawrence, John Keats, Robert Louis Stevenson, Henry David Thoreau, Franz Kafka and George Orwell all died from it. So did Doc Holliday, the gunfighter who teamed with Wyatt Earp at the Battle of the OK Corral in 1881.

It has ravaged people for more than 4,000 years. One of the effects of tuberculosis is that it can eat away large holes in the spine, causing hunched backs that are easy to recognize in skeletons. An Egyptian mummy that dates back to 2400 B.C. was found to have spinal deformities that are one sign of the disease.

The ancient Greeks called it phthisis, which means "slow wasting away." The famous Greek doctor Hippocrates, writing about 460 B.C., said that it was the most prevalent disease of his times. It was almost always fatal. Hippocrates even suggested that doctors should stay away from patients who had an advanced form of the disease.

It was also common during the time of the Roman Empire. Even Peruvian mummies dating back 1,000 years ago—long before the arrival of European invaders—show evidence of tuberculosis.

Infected people often passed the disease on to many others by coughing or sneezing before realizing they were sick. In this way, it spread rapidly from town to town and country to country, a fearsome worldwide plague.

There was no cure.

The English King Charles II, who began his reign in 1660, made popular an old legend that people who suffered from scrofula—tuberculosis of the lymph nodes in the neck—could be healed if a king or queen laid hands on them. Some historians estimate that Charles touched more than 4,000 scrofula victims annually. Other victims went to doctors who tried to treat the disease by "bleeding" their patients. They would cut open the person's veins and let some blood drain out.

Not surprisingly, neither treatment was effective and the disease raged on. What was worse, no one knew what caused it. Some people believed that it was hereditary. Others were convinced that it was the result of a "sinful" lifestyle.

The first ray of hope came in the middle of the 19th century. A young botany student in Silesia (part of modern-day Poland) named Hermann Brehmer contracted tuberculosis. Doctors told him to seek out a healthier climate. He journeyed to the Himalayan Mountains in central Asia. Miraculously, his symptoms disappeared.

When he returned, he began to study medicine and soon built the first sanatorium. Located in the mountains, it provided tuberculosis sufferers with an opportunity to rest in the midst of trees, improve their nutrition and breathe clear, cold, clean air. It become a model for similar institutions that quickly spread throughout Europe and the United States.

Sanitoria were located in cool, dry places because it was believed that this climate helped tuberculosis patients to heal. So did the enforced rest, together with a proper diet and the well-regulated hospital life. Sanitoria provided another function: they isolated the sick, the source of infection, from the general population. That helped to reduce the spread of the disease.

Unfortunately, new patients would normally spend several months of complete bed rest. Even if they grew stronger, they would be separated from their loved ones for one or two years at a time, homesick and lonely while they tried to recover. Despite the isolation and inactivity, however, sanitoria appeared to represent the only potential cure, and they became increasingly popular in the 1900s. At the height of the sanitorium movement in the 1930s, there were more than 600 of them in the U.S. alone, with a total of 84,000 beds.

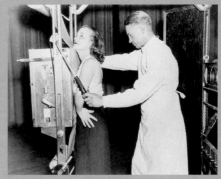

In the early part of the 20th century, the only treatment for tuberculosis was complete bed rest together with controlled nutrition. Hospitals for tuberculosis patients, called sanitoria, were built everywhere. The photograph on the left shows a typical sanitorium in the mountains. The photo on the right shows a patient receiving an x ray to detect tuberculosis.

But in 1882, long before the movement reached its crest, there was a momentous announcement. A German researcher named Robert Koch peered through his microscope and became the first person to see the microorganism that had killed so many people. It was a tiny bacteria, which Koch called *Mycobacterium tuberculosis*. Now that the culprit had been identified, scientists could finally begin studying ways to combat it.

In 1895, another German scientist, Wilhelm Roentgen, discovered X-rays. While they weren't able to prevent tuberculosis, they proved useful in following the course of the disease.

In 1905, Koch was granted the Nobel Prize in Physiology or Medicine for his groundbreaking work. In the lecture that he delivered at the time of receiving his award, he said that "quite an important beginning has been made." But that was all. It was only a beginning.

Robert Koch, shown in this photograph, was a German physician and pioneer bacteriologist who first identified the bacteria that causes tuberculosis. In 1905, Koch won the Nobel Prize for Physiology or Medicine for his groundbreaking work with bacteria.

For in spite of these advances, as the 19th century gave way to the 20th tuberculosis still killed millions of people every year.

Five years after Koch stood before the King of Sweden to receive his Nobel Prize, a young Russian named Selman Waksman stood on the deck of a ship, watching the coastline of Europe fade in the distance. He was on the way to America, where opportunity was boundless.

Waksman didn't know it at the time, but he was also on his way to leading the worldwide race to find the cure for tuberculosis.

That cure lay in a very unlikely location. In the early days of the 20th century, people were starting to believe that diseases could be controlled by cleaning up their surroundings. That meant clean air. Clean food. Clean water. Clean streets.

But Waksman would find the cure in a place where no one had thought to look.

He would find it in dirt.

Selman Waksman grew up in the small Russian village of Novaia-Priluka. Most people from this small town lived there all their lives. Waksman would become an exception, traveling to the United States to settle in New Jersey in 1910.

Chapter 2
A Small Town Boy

● ●

Zolman Abraham Waksman (he later changed his first name to the more American "Selman") was born on July 22, 1888 in the small Russian town of Novaia-Priluka to Jacob and Fradia Waksman. His father was a small property owner and his mother helped in her family's trading and dry-goods business.

Waksman's mother and grandmother had also been born in the town, located in the southwestern corner of what is now the Ukraine. It was 20 miles from the nearest large city, Vinnitsa, where his father and grandfather had been born. Russia in the 1800s was a country where most people lived their whole life in one place. Waksman would be an exception.

"It was a bleak town," he would later write in his autobiography, *My Life with the Microbes*. "It was flat and surrounded by wide, forestless acres. In summer, the fields of wheat, rye, barley, and oats formed an endless sea. In winter, snow covered the ground, and the frosted rivers carried the eye to the boundless horizon, where the skies met the earth somewhere far away."

Although life was hard in Novaia-Priluka, young Selman had a happy childhood. "From my very early childhood, I remember myself as my mother's joy, her hope, and her pride," he recalled. His very name, derived from the ancient Jewish King Solomon, reflected those hopes.

When he was seven, his little sister Miriam was born, but before she could even reach the age of two, she died from diphtheria. There was a cure, but it had to be shipped from Kiev, a city 200 miles away, and it didn't arrive in time to save her life. This tragic event left a strong impression on Selman's mind. For the first time he considered the terrible nature of disease, and the potential for a cure.

"With the death of my sister, my mother spent on me alone all caresses and hopes," he wrote in his autobiography. She wasn't the only one.

"My beloved little grandmother and my many aunts and maiden cousins did their best to spoil me completely," he wrote.

There were no public schools in Waksman's small town, so his mother got her only son the education he needed. Like many people in the town, they were Jewish. Much of his early learning involved reading the Bible and the Talmud in a heder, or private school, which was run by religious authorities. By the time he was 10, his mother employed private tutors, who taught him Hebrew, Russian, literature, history, math, and geography. In the evenings, Waksman would entertain his family with all he had learned.

By age 13, Waksman not only had a deep affection for education, but with the encouragement of his mother, he had also learned to be concerned for the poor. He and three friends opened up their own school, where they invited the underprivileged to come and learn for free, two hours each day. Unlike most of his mother's generation, Waksman believed that education should not just be religious, but should also include grammar, writing, math and history. This experience as a teacher would enable Waksman to earn money as a well-paid tutor and help fund his own education in the coming years.

Despite all these accomplishments, Waksman was still incredibly shy. "I was a bashful youth, who at the sight of a pretty girl would blush to my hairtips!" he confessed in his autobiography. Waksman felt most at home reading books, like the otherworldly stories of Jules Verne and *Robinson Crusoe*. When he had outgrown these, he read Shakespeare and the famous Russian authors Tolstoy and Dostoevski.

But more than anything, Waksman had a thirst for adventure. "I dreamed of the Orinoco and the Amazon Rivers, where I was going to discover new tribes, new herbs, new remedies to cure human ills," he wrote. Even at such an early age, he had the urge to help humankind.

As Selman grew older, he began to realize that he had learned all he could from the opportunities his town had to offer. He knew that in order to keep learning, he would have to leave his home town for a larger city. Although his mother was sad and wished that he would have settled down to marry, she encouraged him nonetheless. His teachers and peers encouraged him too, hoping he would carve out a path that they could follow to a better life.

In Russia in the early 1900s, students in larger cities attended government schools called Gymnasiums and had to pass difficult tests in order to qualify for entrance to a university. Because there was a lot of discrimination against Jews at this time in Russia, they were prevented by the government from receiving an official education at a Gymnasium. The only way to take the Gymnasium test was as an extern, an extra student who was tutored privately. The teachers who gave the tests favored their own students over the externs, whom they had never met.

Waksman's small-town upbringing and Jewish descent put him at a great disadvantage. Only two or three students from his home town had ever passed the Gymnasium exam, and these were children of the rich, who could afford a superb education and years of preparation.

Still, he would not be dissuaded. "I had a legal right to be examined," he wrote in his autobiography.

To prepare for the test, Waksman found a tutor in his town to help him. At age 19, after a year of intensive study, he left for the city of Zhitomir where he rented a room and hired a teacher to help him with the final phases of study.

The exams were incredibly thorough, lasting two weeks, each day covering a different subject. Students were required to pass each exam. One failed test meant you had failed it entirely. Waksman had aced them all, until, on the last day, he was tested in geography, which he called "my beloved subject. I felt more sure of passing that examination than any other."

Waksman answered the first question correctly, but the second question stumped him. The teacher, who looked down upon him because he was from a small, unknown town, asked him to identify the river in the city of Berlin. Waksman knew all the major rivers in Germany, and his adventurous mind had dreamt many times of riding boats along the Rhine, the Elbe, the Oder, the Moselle, the Danube. In comparison to these mighty watercourses, what flowed through Berlin was little more than a trickle. But he couldn't remember its name.

The teacher gave Waksman a zero, and with that, he had to wait two years to retake the exam. Years later, visiting Berlin as a successful young scientist, Waksman would stand on a bridge spanning that river, wondering how his life might have been different if he had remembered that it was called the Spree.

Severely disappointed, he returned home. His peers were even more discouraged than he was. If he couldn't make it, what chance did they have? But Waksman refused to give up. He used his funds from tutoring to move to Odessa, a large seaport city almost 400 miles from Priluka where he could hire teachers who were even better. Odessa was a great cultural and educational center, and it opened a whole new world for Waksman and filled him with hope for the future. He and his best friend from childhood, Peisi, studied day and night. Finally, the time came to take the Gymnasium again. This time, Waksman passed, and came home a hero.

But his triumph would not last long. Soon after his return home, his dear mother suddenly became gravely ill. She died two weeks later, with Selman at her bedside. At age 22, with his mother gone, he wanted nothing but to run away from it all. His father had remarried, and Selman couldn't stand the thought of a different woman in the house.

He also couldn't stand the thought of remaining in Russia, where he would have to deal not only with the lack of personal freedom but also with prejudice against Jews. So when cousins in America invited him to join them, he was receptive to the idea.

In mid-October of 1910, Selman, Peisi and several others left Priluka by train for the German border. From there, they boarded a ship for Philadelphia, where they landed on November 2, 1910, with high hopes for a better life in the New World.

When Selman Waksman first immigrated to the United States, he settled in Metuchen, New Jersey, and soon enrolled at Rutgers College (now Rutgers University) to study agriculture.

Chapter 3

Success in the New World

•••

Selman quickly settled in with his cousin Molki and her husband, Mendel Kornblatt—a distant cousin of Selman—who lived on a small farm in Metuchen, New Jersey. Waksman spent his first few months there, working under the guidance of Mendel. A farm was the perfect place for Selman Waksman to begin life in America. It was here that he watched things grow for the first time, learning the life processes of plants and animals.

At Mendel's prompting, he traveled the few miles to Rutgers College in New Brunswick. There he met with Dr. Jacob G. Lipman, another Russian immigrant, who would soon become the dean of the College of Agriculture. Lipman was immediately fond of Selman, and offered him the opportunity to study at the college. But Selman wasn't sure.

On the basis of his Gymnasium exams, he had been accepted to the College of Physicians and Surgeons at Columbia, in New York. Should he study medicine or agriculture? The decision would be a fateful one.

Waksman considered the large amount of money that would be required for an education in medicine, money he didn't have. He thought about how fascinated he'd been by the mysteries of plant and animal life he witnessed working on the farm. He remembered his youth and the comforting aroma of the soil in Priluka.

There was one other consideration.

"I was becoming more and more saturated with the spirit of the New World—a desire to depend on myself," he wrote.

Influenced by these things and Dr. Lipman's advice, Waksman wanted to enroll at Rutgers. But with virtually no money, he needed a scholarship so he could attend, and scholarships were only awarded on the basis of competitive examinations.

Once again, he faced an examination that would determine his future. Once again, he failed one portion, this one dealing with English literature. But this was the New World. He received his scholarship, with one condition: he had to take the English literature test again and pass it. He did.

However, fitting in at Rutgers was not easy. Waksman was used to being the youngest in his classes, and now he was 23, with peers who were all between 17 and 20. To make matters worse, he knew nothing of sports, a pastime that obsessed many of his fellow students. Add to this his struggle to learn the English language, and one can only imagine how hard it must have been for him.

But instead of giving up, he focused all his energy on learning. He especially loved his science courses. Their hands-on laboratory experiments were something he had never been able to do before. In turn, his professors were impressed by his energy and eagerness to learn, and some even gave him extra opportunities to gain more knowledge.

Meanwhile, Waksman worked on Mendel's farm to earn his keep. But he lost considerable time traveling back and forth to school, time he would prefer to spend in the lab and reading in the library. At the end of his sophomore year he decided to leave the farm and take a job with Dr. Byron Halsted, a master botanist. He moved into an old house at the College Farm for three dollars a month, and worked there for 20 cents an hour, helping Dr. Halsted in the lab on rainy days.

Dr. Halsted was very fond of Selman, and trusted him to oversee many of his personal studies and experiments. He spent many hours with Selman analyzing scientific methods, teaching him about plant genetics—the study of how plants develop—and many other topics that weren't job-related at all. And he insisted that Selman report all the hours that they spent together as having worked for him, for he knew that the young man needed the money. They grew to become very close friends.

Although college life had been difficult for Waksman at first, his dedication and thirst for knowledge soon paid off. He had completed all the necessary credits to graduate by his junior year, and was able to spend his last year of college on a research problem of his choosing. He worked side by side with graduate students, who had already finished college and were continuing their studies, at the New Jersey Agricultural Experiment Station on campus.

Every month throughout the year, Waksman dug several trenches at different parts of the College Farm. His goal was to count the colonies, or groups, of bacteria that lived in each of several distinct layers of soil that his digging exposed. However, he also found fungus colonies. And to his surprise, he discovered a third group of microorganisms, somewhere between bacteria and fungi. This was his first encounter with what would become his life's passion: a group of microbes in the soil called actinomycetes, which had been almost entirely overlooked in previous research.

Waksman graduated in 1915, with a Bachelor of Science degree in agriculture. By this time he was sure that his strongest interest was in soil microbiology, the study of the various tiny life forms that lived in the soil.

Dr. Halsted had a graduation gift for him. Selman had recently been elected to Phi Beta Kappa, the national scholastic honorary. Dr. Halsted pulled a five-dollar gold piece from his pocket, telling Selman to take it to a jeweler and have it made into a key that was the symbol of Phi Beta Kappa.

"I was so overcome with emotion that I could only utter a few words in reply," Selman said in his autobiography.

Dr. Lipman invited the new graduate to become a research assistant in his department. He would continue his senior year's research on the actinomycetes at the New Jersey Agricultural Station and work toward a Master of Science degree.

Selman spent nearly every waking moment at the lab, but he still found time for fun. On weekends he would visit his old friend Peisi in New York.

But seeing Peisi wasn't the only reason he liked going to New York. The rest of Peisi's family had followed the two young men to America. The family included Peisi's younger sister, Bobili (whose real name was Bertha Deborah Mitnik) and Waksman was in love with her.

When he earned his masters degree, Selman was ready to move on. He received a fellowship to attend the University of California at Berkeley. To understand all the complex interrelations that occurred in soil microbiology, he needed further training in chemistry, and especially biochemistry— the study of chemical reactions in living things.

"I had sent my roots into the soil," he remembered in his autobiography. "I was on my way. I knew now exactly what I wanted and how to get it."

One thing that he wanted was Bobili. They were married on the morning of August 4, 1916, had lunch together at a restaurant, then packed everything into two suitcases and headed for California. To save money, they traveled each night on a train so they didn't have to pay a hotel bill, then spent the following day sightseeing.

In California, Selman earned his Ph.D., or doctor of philosophy degree, in biochemistry in 1918. He did well out west and could have remained, especially since he and his wife found that people there generally were much friendlier than back east.

But he wanted to return to soil microbiology. And unlike many people who moved to California because of its mild climate, Selman missed the heavy snows and ice he had encountered while he was growing up. So he moved back to the East Coast with an even more solid grasp of microorganisms and their life processes. He was immediately appointed to a position of lecturer in soil microbiology at Rutgers.

On September 15, 1919, Bobili gave birth to what would become the couple's only child. There was no question about what they would name him: Byron Halsted Waksman, in honor of Selman's teacher, who had recently died.

The years that followed were an incredible period of growth for Waksman.

In 1924, he and Bobili saved enough money for a world tour, meeting with famous scientists to trade knowledge. It would be the first of many trips abroad.

In 1926 he became an assistant professor at Rutgers.

The following year, the young Russian who had failed his Gymnasium exams for being unable to remember the name of a Berlin river published a 900-page textbook, *Principles of Soil Microbiology.* The world now looked at Waksman as the leading authority on his subject, and his book as the definitive publication on the topic.

Rene Dubos, shown in this picture, was a student of Selman Waksman's at Rutgers. He was inspired by Waksman's research into soil microorganisms. After he received his Ph.D. at Rutgers, he went to work at the Rockefeller Institute in New York. There, working side by side with medical researchers, he discovered the first substance ever found by purposefully testing soil microorganisms that had a destructive effect on disease-causing bacteria. With Dubos' discovery, Waksman began to think about the possible human benefits of the microbes he'd been studying.

Four years later he would become a full professor. By now, he had also embarked on what he would term his "humus period," a decade-long concentration on the soil element that produced nutrients for plants.

"All my efforts focused on the microbiological population of the soil, its nature and activities, and especially its role in soil fertility, specifically the decomposition of human, animal and plant wastes," he said. His work included five trips to Europe and produced many honors from national and international bodies. Perhaps even more important, it had helped to establish microbiology as an important field of science.

"I thus completed the fifth decade of my life with an established reputation in my selected science," he noted.

Under normal circumstances, he continued, it would have been "the culminating point of all my previous preparation, of all my plans and hopes."

But it wasn't.

The next decade would produce results that were far beyond his wildest imagination. It began when one of his students, a young scientist named René Dubos, would make a discovery that would change the course of Waksman's research. In doing so, it would alter the course of history.

Shortly before World War II broke out, Selman Waksman (left) met Alexander Fleming at the Third International Congress for Microbiology. Fleming, who had discovered penicillin's antibiotic properties in 1928, inspired Waksman. All of a sudden, the huge potential of microorganisms became clear to him. From that moment on, he devoted himself to the search for antibiotics.

Chapter 4

Inspiration and Disappointment

Dubos had been among Waksman's first students, and at first, he did not stand out. But eventually Waksman suspected that there was something special about him. He was right. Dubos worked hard and learned as much as he could from Waksman. After receiving his Ph.D. from Rutgers in 1927, he moved to New York to work at the prestigious Rockefeller Institute. It was there, in 1939, that he made a monumental discovery.

Dubos was trying to fight one of the deadliest bacteria in the world, the staphylococcus. It caused blood poisoning, boils, and deadly wound infections. In Dubos' time, if you were infected with this bacteria, there was little hope. He tested thousands of different microorganisms in the soil to see if any could kill the staphylococcus bacteria. He found a microbe that could, called *Bacillus brevis*. The drug produced from *Bacillus brevis*, called gramicidin, proved to be too poisonous for humans to swallow, but it was successful in treating skin infections with creams and nose and sinus infections with nasal sprays.

The importance of Dubos' discovery was that it was the first substance ever found by purposefully testing soil microorganisms that had a destructive effect on disease-causing bacteria. Unlike Dubos, who worked side by side with medical researchers at the Rockefeller Institute, Waksman was not medically trained. The microbes that live in soil were Waksman's passion. He never thought of them in terms of curing human diseases.

But with Dubos' discovery, Waksman began to think about the possible human benefits of the microbes he'd been studying. He soon coined the term "antibiotic" to describe any organism that has a harmful effect on another organism.

World War II was about to break out, and Selman knew that it would be likely to cause widespread infections and epidemics. These would require new ways of treatment.

But it wasn't until September of that year, at the Third International Congress for Microbiology, that Waksman was convinced to take action.

It was there that he met Alexander Fleming, who had recently discovered penicillin, an extremely effective antibiotic created from a mold. Although penicillin proved useless against tuberculosis, it worked wonders against many different types of bacteria.

The huge potential of microorganisms was suddenly clear to Waksman. His mission was clear. From that moment on, he would devote himself to the search for antibiotics. When he returned from the conference, he rushed to the lab and declared to his assistants, "Drop everything!"

Waksman's research had taken a sharp turn. But he was still not ready to tackle the challenge of finding an antibiotic to treat tuberculosis. Instead, he and his research team focused on a group of bacteria called the Gram-negatives. These bacteria were deadly, reeking destruction on the body and costing millions of lives a year. But neither Dubos' gramicidin nor Fleming's penicillin were effective against them. Could the solution be in the soil?

Waksman was sure of it. "The stakes were high," he remembered in his autobiography. "And the game seemed worth the chance."

He immediately set up a system to search for microbes that might kill these dangerous Gram-negatives. This system involved layering a sample of Gram-negative bacteria over a sample of soil. If antibacterial microbes were present in the soil, a clear circle would form where the bacteria had been killed. Using this method, almost at once Waksman and his team discovered a microbe that killed Gram-negative bacteria. Their plan had worked! They named this newly discovered microorganism "actinomycin."

A frenzied energy took over the lab. Waksman was going to change the face of modern medicine! He would later write in his autobiography: "Who can forget the excitement of those days? It was like immersing oneself in a whirlpool of new ideas."

But his hopes were dashed almost as soon as they had been raised. Actinomycin never made it past animal testing. Even in small amounts it proved to be so toxic that it killed mice within two days.

Still, Waksman continued his search, this time with the help of the nearby pharmaceutical company Merck & Co. By this time, many of Waksman's assistants were given no other duties but to test actinomycetes microbes. Sure enough, another anti-bacterial drug called streptothricin was found in 1942. Animals were dramatically cured of infection and for the second time, the spirits of the lab were sent soaring.

However, heartbreak was about to strike again. Just before the human trials were to begin, animals who had been given streptothricin suddenly died. The drug had caused a delayed toxicity and could not be used in humans.

Waksman was disappointed, of course. But his optimism was unfailing. "The horizons were now unlimited," he remembered in his autobiography. "New fields were opened. Was it not time to attack the most difficult of all infectious diseases, tuberculosis?"

In 1943, Selman Waksman led a team of Rutgers University researchers that isolated streptomycin, the first antibiotic effective against tuberculosis in humans. Waksman was encouraged by the findings of one of his students, Rene Dubos, whose work led to the discovery in 1939 of gramicidin, the first clinically useful topical antibiotic. Waksman put his graduate students and assistants to work looking for antibiotics. In 1943, Albert Schatz, a student of Waksman's isolated streptomycin.

Chapter 5

The Search for a Cure

By 1943, the world needed a cure for tuberculosis more than ever. With the poverty, stress and struggle brought on by World War II, tuberculosis was on the rise across the globe. In the early 1940s, the Great White Plague was affecting five million lives a year.

This was the situation when Waksman took up the task of finding a treatment. But what had convinced him to hunt for an antibiotic to kill tuberculosis then, in 1943, and not from the outset of his antibiotic research? After all, prior to Waksman's moment of inspiration, evidence had been gathering that organisms in the soil could harm the tuberculosis bacteria.

In 1932, the American Tuberculosis Society asked Waksman to perform an experiment to see if tuberculosis germs could survive in normal soil. Waksman gave the assignment to one of his assistants, Chester Rhines. Rhines discovered that if tuberculosis bacteria were added to certain types of soil, they died. Shouldn't this have sparked even a glimmer of hope in Waksman's mind? Maybe, but at that point Waksman had not even begun his antibiotics research.

"My general impression at that time was that these results seemed to lead nowhere," he stated in a book he later wrote about his discovery of streptomycin, called *The Conquest of Tuberculosis*. "In the scientific climate of the time, the results did not suggest any practical applications for the treatment of tuberculosis."

A year later, an associate who worked in the Poultry Department at Rutgers brought a test tube of tuberculosis

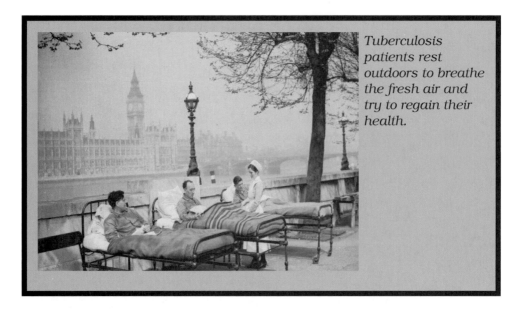

Tuberculosis patients rest outdoors to breathe the fresh air and try to regain their health.

bacteria that had been killed by mold to Waksman. But again, Waksman didn't investigate further. He had even received a letter from his son, Byron, after the antibiotics search had begun. Byron, inspired by his father's research, suggested that he try to find antibiotic substances that might harm tuberculosis bacteria. Waksman's reply was "The time has not come yet. We are not quite prepared to undertake this problem. But we are rapidly approaching it."

There were other reasons for Waksman's hesitancy. For one, he didn't have the proper resources. His laboratory was small, and designed for studying soil. Another factor was money, or lack of it. It would have been very costly to investigate potential antibiotics for tuberculosis, and Waksman couldn't get funding.

But on June 1, 1943, at a meeting in New York to discuss the problems of treating tuberculosis, everything would change. Like the inspiration that had triggered Waksman's search for antibiotics four years earlier, this meeting of minds would aim him straight at his greatest success: a treatment for tuberculosis.

That moment grew from Waksman's frustration at a colleague at the conference who had suggested that a cure might be found in a certain enzyme derived from an earthworm. Waksman thought the idea was absurd, and said so. His colleague angrily answered back, "How do you propose to go about this problem?"

And it was then that Waksman knew. "The antibiotics will do it," he said. "Just give us time."

Selman Waksman poses in his lab in New Brunswick, New Jersey on November 26, 1952.

Waksman worked on many experiments in his laboratory at Rutgers and inspired his graduate students and assistants to help in his search for an antibiotic to conquer tuberculosis.

Chapter 6

The Great Discovery

W aksman had many assistants working for him in his lab, but none was brighter or more dedicated than Albert Schatz, who joined just as Waksman had set his sights on tuberculosis. It was a search Schatz could identify with, since he remembered losing friends and family who had suffered from the disease when he was in his youth. He witnessed them slowly waste away, with no cure in sight. Now, under the direction of Waksman, Schatz had the opportunity to do something about it.

Waksman and his new assistant were very close. Waksman trusted Schatz and let him work quite independently. In turn, Schatz looked up to Waksman and came to him with various problems and questions in his research. Taking what he had learned from the discovery of the first two antibiotics—actinomycin and streptothricin—Waksman was confident that the antibiotic that would kill the tuberculosis bacteria would come from the actinomycetes. Schatz worked day and night, testing these strange half-bacterial, half-fungal microbes wherever he could find them.

Finally, on October 19, 1943, three months after Schatz had begun his experiments, four hard years after Waksman had begun his search for antibiotics, and centuries after the only hope for the sick was the possibility of a king's healing touch, the miracle had been found. The greenish-gray organism Schatz held on a plate in his hand would produce streptomycin.

But Waksman was wary. He didn't want to get his hopes up again only to find that, like the other drugs they discovered, streptomycin would also be too poisonous. However, holding back excitement was hard. In every test they conducted, streptomycin showed more dramatic results than the other two antibiotics, leaving large clear circles where the bacteria had once been. It was also effective not just against tuberculosis but against many other Gram-negative bacteria against which penicillin was useless.

The next step was purifying the chemical. The microbe needed to be diluted in a liquid, either ether or water, so that it could be injected into animals and, eventually, humans. Schatz did what he could, working day and night in the lab and even sleeping there, trying to concentrate the antibiotic for testing. But this was a job for specially-trained chemists, and the soil microbiology lab wasn't properly equipped. Large amounts of the drug would be needed for testing and it had to be made quickly. Waksman called on Merck & Co., who had collaborated with him to produce and test streptothrycin, to do the job.

Now they were ready to test streptomycin on animals, but again, the humble lab did not have the resources. Waksman and Schatz had published their remarkable discovery in a scientific journal in April of 1944. Luckily, it drew the attention of Dr. William H. Feldman and Dr. H. Corwin Hinshaw of the Mayo Clinic, a medical center in Minnesota. The timing was perfect. The two men had been using other drugs to try to cure tuberculosis but none were successful. Now they wanted to test streptomycin on animals.

Feldman and Hinshaw performed the first experiment on guinea pigs infected with tuberculosis on April 27, 1944. They treated four with streptomycin, and used eight as controls, or animals who did not receive streptomycin so

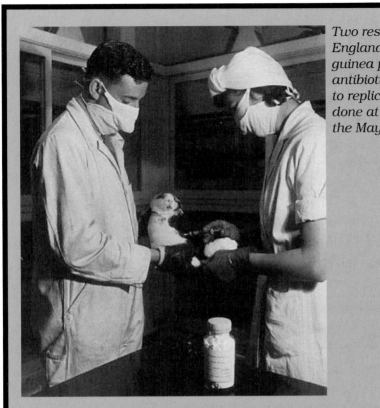

Two researchers in England inject a guinea pig with the antibiotic streptomycin to replicate the studies done at Rutgers and the Mayo Clinic.

they could be used for comparison. Would the antibiotic be effective? Would it be too toxic and kill the animals? Feldman and Hinshaw waited eagerly. What they found thrilled them beyond anything they had ever witnessed. The four guinea pigs who had been given streptomycin were cured of tuberculosis five days later.

Larger scale experiments followed, and the results were astonishing. Guinea pigs with blood-borne tuberculosis, a fatal type of tuberculosis where the bacteria gets into the bloodstream and attacks the entire body, were completely healed. Even more incredible, no side effects of the drug or the disease could be seen.

The final and most important step had arrived—it was time to test streptomycin on humans.

But what was the correct dosage and what would the possible side effects be? Since nobody had ever treated tuberculosis patients with streptomycin before, it was a guessing game. But Patricia, a 21-year-old woman suffering from pulmonary tuberculosis, or tuberculosis of the lungs, was willing to take the chance. Patricia was very sick. After a year in a sanitorium, she had seen no improvement, suffering from a racking cough, chills, and high fever.

In November of 1944, at the Mayo Clinic, Feldman and Hinshaw treated Patricia with streptomycin. Even though the drug was not yet available in a steady supply and Patricia's treatment had to be interrupted several times when the streptomycin ran out, improvements were seen almost immediately. Her temperature went down and she began the slow process of healing.

The Mayo Clinic in Rochester, Minnesota, helped Waksman test streptomycin.

These bottles show the different stages of the streptomycin antibiotic. To begin with, streptomycin griseus is bred in bottles and after the 14th day, the mold that has grown is removed and the streptomycin has passed into the liquid.

"It is a happy ending which has been duplicated tens of thousands of times in the streptomycin story," said one of Hinshaw's assistants. "The patient made a remarkable recovery." Patricia went on to get married, have children, and lead a normal life.

From that moment on, the production of streptomycin and treatment on humans began at a very rapid pace. Many more tests were conducted, all with similarly thrilling results. In 1946, Feldman and Hinshaw sent a telegram to Waksman, confirming that streptomycin was indeed the first effective remedy for tuberculosis. They ended the note, "Hearty congratulations."

Indeed! For the first time in history, there was a drug to treat the Great White Plague. "The control of tuberculosis may finally materialize and thus advance man one step further in his battle against disease and epidemics," Waksman stated in his book *The Conquest of Tuberculosis.* "Streptomycin pointed the way." The experiment by the American Tuberculosis Society in 1932 had been on the right track. The first effective treatment for tuberculosis had come from the soil.

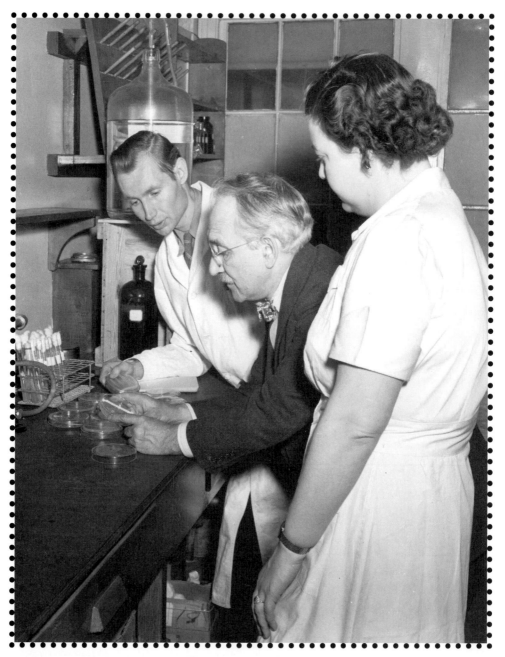

Selman Waksman had several enthusiastic assistants and graduate students who enjoyed the challenges he presented to them.

Chapter 7
Saving Lives

● ●

I n 1947, streptomycin was finally made available to the public. Its fame spread rapidly. The drug worked miraculous results in several types of tuberculosis that were almost always fatal, including tuberculous meningitis and blood-borne tuberculosis. It was also extremely effective in many other forms of the disease, including pulmonary tuberculosis such as Patricia's.

During the next 10 years, death rates dropped considerably. Streptomycin conferences were being held twice a year, and clinics and hospitals throughout the world were working together to gather information on the uses of the drug. The world had come together to combat tuberculosis on a scale never before seen in the history of medicine.

But there were still problems. For one, demand greatly outweighed supply. "Desperate patients, their relatives, and physicians from many countries throughout the world sought to obtain streptomycin when none was to be had," remembered Hinshaw. Unfortunately, resources were not yet available to manufacture the drug at the necessary rate. Waksman and Hinshaw were flooded with letters begging for streptomycin to save their loved ones. Nothing was more heartbreaking to Waksman than to know that the drug could not reach all those who needed it. But with each letter of desperation, he received many letters of thanks from those whose lives had been saved by streptomycin.

"How can I describe the impressions left upon me by the first sight of a child, no matter in what country and in what position in life, who had been saved from certain death by the use of a drug in the discovery of which I had played but a humble part?" he wrote in *The Conquest of Tuberculosis*.

Streptomycin was a success, without a doubt. But it was not perfect. The drug was toxic to a small percentage of patients, causing deafness or the loss of balance. But as one father whose daughter had been saved by streptomycin stated, "I'd rather have a deaf child than a dead child." As time passed, doctors learned the best dosages to treat patients so that the fewest possible people suffered from these side effects.

Still, there was another, bigger problem facing streptomycin. The tuberculosis bacteria had the tendency to grow a resistance to the drug after several months of treatment. When this happened, the drug was no longer effective in killing the bacteria, and patients could suffer a relapse. However, when Waksman discovered streptomycin, he had done more than just find one drug. His discovery flung open the gates to the possibilities of treating tuberculosis with antibiotics, and scientists across the world followed his lead.

Soon after streptomycin, two other very important drugs were discovered. These drugs, PAS (para-aminosalicylic acid) and isoniazid, began to be used with streptomycin to treat tuberculosis. Patients received either two or three of the drugs at the same time. This method was highly effective in preventing the bacteria from becoming resistant to any one drug. It was this combination treatment that knocked tuberculosis to its knees.

Hinshaw reported in 1955 that in the ten years previous, "a 75 percent reduction in deaths from tuberculosis had been accomplished in the United States."

With the death toll dropping, the need for sanitoria dwindled as well. All across the country and the world, these once overcrowded hospitals were shutting their doors.

"The closing of the famous Trudeau Sanitorium has made many people more aware than any figures could of the events taking place in the field of tuberculosis therapy," Waksman stated in *The Conquest of Tuberculosis*.

In May of 1952, five years after streptomycin had been made public and nine years after the landmark drug had been discovered, an institute of microbiology was built at Rutgers in Waksman's honor. What better place to erect the building than on the site of the old agricultural college where his discovery had been made? As soon as he heard the news, he and his wife Bobili built a house nearby, so he could always be close to the institute. For Waksman, it was the culmination of years of hard work.

As if this were not enough, several months later Waksman received the news that he had won the Nobel Prize for Medicine or Physiology. He was flooded with congratulations from all over the world. Friends, colleagues, former students, and tuberculosis patients wrote and called to acknowledge his accomplishment.

However, his excitement was soon dampened. The Nobel Prize Committee had awarded the honor to Waksman alone, and had excluded Albert Schatz, the assistant who played such an important role in the discovery of streptomycin and who was once a dear friend of Waksman.

Schatz argued that he should also receive the prize, and the issue erupted into a huge controversy in the scientific community. But many scientists believed that since Waksman orchestrated the entire antibiotic program, he was responsible for the discovery of streptomycin, and should receive the prize alone. The Nobel Prize Committee stuck to the original decision.

On December 12, 1952, Waksman traveled to Sweden to receive the Nobel Prize. In the congratulatory speech, Professor A. Wallgren of the Royal Caroline Institute, who awards the prize, declared, "Streptomycin has already saved thousands of human lives. As physicians, we regard you as one of the greatest benefactors to mankind."

Selman Waksman's career was indeed a long and accomplished one. The research program in his department went on to discover more than 30 antibiotics and anti-cancer drugs, among them neomycin and candicidin. Waksman published more than 500 papers and 28 books in his lifetime. In 1958, he retired as director of the institute of microbiology, and spent his later years researching the microbes of the sea, helping to organize the Division of Marine Bacteriology at the Woods Hole Oceanographic Institution.

On August 16, 1973, at the age of 85, Selman Waksman died. In his honor, the institute of microbiology at Rutgers College was soon named after him.

Although tuberculosis has not been eradicated, streptomycin, in combination with other drugs, is still effective in its treatment. It is also useful in fighting other infectious diseases caused by bacteria.

But Waksman was more than just the mastermind behind this one drug. He was a pioneer of the antibiotic revolution. The poor boy from a small town in Russia had taken his passion for the soil and turned it into a medical miracle. As he once told a reporter, "Out of the earth shall come thy salvation."

Selman Waksman Chronology

1888 born on July 8 in Novaia-Priluka, Russia

1901 opens school for the poor in Novaia-Priluka

1907 moves to Zhitomir and takes Gymnasium exams for first time

1909 moves to Odessa and passes Gymnasium exams on second try; mother dies suddenly

1910 leaves Russia and arrives in United States

1911 enrolls at Rutgers College in New Brunswick, N.J.

1913 begins working with master botanist Dr. Byron Halsted and moves onto campus

1914 begins research in actinomycetes

1915 receives bachelor of science degree, works at Rutgers as research assisant and later with Department of Agriculture in Washington, D.C.

1916 earns masters degree, marries Bertha Deborah Mitnik and moves to California

1918 receives Ph.D. degree in biochemistry and returns to Rutgers to accept position as lecturer in soil microbiology.

1919 son Byron is born

1924 embarks on world tour to exchange ideas with fellow scientists

1926 appointed assistant professor at Rutgers

1927 publishes textbook *Principles of Soil Microbiology*

1939 begins to think about human benefits of microbes

1940 discovers actinomycin

1942 discovers streptothricin

1943 working with Albert Schatz, discovers streptomycin

1944 publishes discovery with Schatz in scientific journal

1949 discovers neomycin

1952 institute of microbiology built in his honor

1952 wins Nobel Prize in Physiology or Medicine for discovery of streptomycin

1973 dies on August 16

1974 institute of microbiology named after him

Tuberculosis Timeline

2400 B.C. people die of tuberculosis, as evidenced by skeletal remains of Egyptian mummies

460 B.C. Greek doctor Hippocrates writes that phthisis ("slow wasting away") is the most common disease of the times

1546 Girolamo Tracastoro's book *De Morbis Contagiosis* is first published work to reveal contagious nature of tuberculosis

1720 English doctor Benjamin Marten suggests that tuberculosis might be caused by "wonderfully minute living creatures"

1854 Hermann Brehmer builds world's first sanitorium following his recovery from tuberculosis

1865 French physician Jean-Antoine demonstrates that tuberculosis can be passed from humans to cattle, and from cattle to rabbits

1882 Robert Koch discovers that tuberculosis is caused by bacteria

1885 Edward Trudeau establishes what becomes most famous U.S. sanitorium, in Saranac Lake, New York

1895 German scientist Wilhelm Roentgen discovers X-rays, which are useful in following the course of tuberculosis

1908 French scientists Albert Calmette and Camille Guerin develop vaccine for use against tuberculosis, but its value is very limited

1928 Alexander Fleming discovers penicillin

1932 American Tuberculosis Society asks Waksman to investigate TB germs in soil

1939 Rene Dubos discovers *Bacillus brevis* by purposefully testing soil microorganisms, which results in first antibiotic ever found

1943 working with Albert Schatz, Waksman discovers streptomycin, the first effective treatment for tuberculosis

1944 Dr. William Feldman and Dr. Corwin Hinshaw of Mayo Clinic test streptomycin on animals and later treat their first human patient

1947 streptomycin made available to public

1973 The use of BCG, a vaccine against tuberculosis, is distributed worldwide

1985 Rate of tuberculosis cases in the U.S. increases for the first time since 1950s

1986 Outbreak of TB cases in New York City among homeless and HIV-positive

1990 Strain W is discovered, a strain of TB that is resistant to numerous drugs

2001 Global Alliance for TB drug development, a nonprofit partnership takes on the challenge to develop new drugs to fight drug-resistant strains of TB

2002 June, 4th World TB Congress reaffirms need for more R&D efforts to conquer new strains of TB.

Further Reading

On the Web

http://info.rutgers.edu/University/alumni/HDA2/waksman.html

http://waksman.rutgers.edu/Waks/Waksman/history.html

http://scienceweek.com/search/reports1/kawudym.htm

http://www.hippocrates.com/archive/December2000/12departments/
12greatmoments.html

http://nobel.se/medicine/laureates/1952/waksman-bio.html

http://jama.ama-assn.org/issues/v282n11/ffull/jwr0915-2.html

http://waksman.rutgers.edu/Waks/Waksman/DrWaksman.html

http://www.who.int/infectious-disease-report/2000/ch2.htm

http://www.nobel.se/medicine/laureates/1952/press.html

Books

Daniel, Thomas M. *Captain of Death: The Story of Tuberculosis.* Rochester, NY: Boydell and Brewer, 1999.

Hyde, Margaret O. *Know About Tuberculosis.* New York: Walker and Company, 1994.

Ryan, Frank, M.D. *The Forgotten Plague.* Boston: Little, Brown and Company, 1993.

Waksman, Selman. *The Conquest of Tuberculosis.* Berkeley: University of California Press, 1964.

Waksman, Selman. *My Life With the Microbes.* New York: Simon and Schuster, 1954.

Glossary

actinomycetes – microorganisms halfway in evolution between fungi and bacteria

antibiotic – organism that has a harmful effect on another organism

fungi – spore-bearing plants that include yeasts, molds, mildews and mushrooms

Gram-negative bacteria – bacteria that fail to stain with a dye invented by Danish bacteriologist Hans Christian Gram

microorganism – an organism too small to see without a microscope

plague - a highly contagious disease that quickly affects a great many people

streptomycin – an antibiotic used to treat tuberculosis and other infectious diseases

Index

PIUTE MIDDLE SCHOOL
Lancaster School District
44711 N. Cedar Ave.
Lancaster, CA 93534